TROY MODEL CLUB SERIES

RECENT LOCOMOTIVES (1947-70)

RECENT LOCOMOTIVES (1947-70)

P. E. Randall

NELSON

THOMAS NELSON AND SONS LIMITED
36 Park Street London W 1
PO Box 27 Lusaka
PO Box 18123 Nairobi
PO Box 21149 Dar es Salaam
77 Coffee Street San Fernando Trinidad
THOMAS NELSON (AUSTRALIA) LIMITED
597 Little Collins Street Melbourne 3000
THOMAS NELSON AND SONS (CANADA) LIMITED
81 Curlew Drive Don Mills Ontario
THOMAS NELSON (NIGERIA) LIMITED
PO Box 336 Apapa Lagos
THOMAS NELSON AND SONS (SOUTH AFRICA) (PROPRIETARY) LIMITED
51 Commissioner Street Johannesburg

First published 1970
SBN 17 213209 6

Photography by Michael Langford

Printed and bound by SIR JOSEPH CAUSTON AND SONS LTD *London and Eastleigh*

CONTENTS

This book is dedicated to the late Frank Hornby,
whose products gave pleasure to countless numbers
of boys of the author's generation.

Many people have helped me with the book, but I should like to single out a few whose assistance has been invaluable. My grateful thanks go to Peter Gomm, my partner and collaborator in many model railway matters, to his firm, Messrs Bold and Burrows, and to Gordon Buttress, for the loan of models; to my good friend Ray Riisnaes, for his help and advice in areas where there were gaps in my knowledge; to Michael Langford, without whose brilliant and dedicated photographic work this book could not have been published.

Finally I feel that this would be an appropriate place to record my great debt to Meccano Ltd (now Meccano Triang Ltd) whose various products have given me pleasure and relaxation for forty-five years, and still continue to do so.

INTRODUCTION

THE POST-WAR YEARS

On the railways, both here and abroad, the post-war years were a time of great change. Britain had been affected by shortages and enemy action, and, at the end of the war, many of the locomotives on its railways were beginning to show signs of age. Steam power was still almost universal, although it had long disappeared from the roads. The four main companies then so familiar—the London, Midland and Scottish; the London and North Eastern; the Great Western; and the Southern—had barely had time to formulate their programmes when nationalization came about. Unlike many of his fellow railway enthusiasts, the author thought this step logical, inevitable and highly desirable. It did mean, however, that, except for a few minor locomotives, the new post-war range of motive power was born entirely under British Railways' ownership.

Many fine steam locomotives were built in the 1950s, but all were to disappear in 1967 and 1968 because the policy of using only diesel and electric motive power was very quickly implemented. Again the author considers this a correct and inevitable policy, although he can appreciate that, for the enthusiast, something was lost when steam disappeared from British Railways.

Model locomotives naturally followed a pattern similar to the real locomotives, with one important exception. Although models exist now of most of the main diesel and electric locos, nostalgia is satisfied by an equally wide range of the older steam-powered engines. Triang are now producing models of very old engines such as the *Rocket*, and they are also making their more modern items optionally available in the old company colours. At the time of writing, therefore, a position exists which is quite unique, enabling an enthusiast to model either the trains of today or of yesterday.

MODEL LOCOMOTIVES

It has also been a time of change both in the size and style of the model railways and the material of which they are made. Before the war, 'O' gauge (1¼ inches rail width) was the most popular size and '1' gauge (1¾ inches) was still very much alive. A smaller size, 'OO' gauge (⅝ inch) had just appeared on the scene as a commercial proposition and was becoming more popular.

When the war ended all the toy factories were, of course, on essential work, and this continued until about 1946 or 1947. When they were finally allowed to return to making toys, raw materials were still controlled and all, especially metal, were in very short supply. As might be expected, the toy-makers first produced trains that were virtually identical with those they had produced prior to 1939. But times had changed. No-one had large attics to spare for model railways, and most rooms were being lived in, as there was a great housing shortage. Clearly the only space for a model railway was to be found in a corner of a bedroom or on a portable baseboard. Now in such a space only a very simple layout is possible in 'O' gauge, so boys, and their fathers, turned to the smaller scales. Space was not the only reason for this, however, for boys were becoming more sophisticated and demanding realistic working layouts. No longer was the familiar oval or circle of track acceptable. Stations, sidings and loop lines were wanted. So even if a fair-sized room was available, people still turned to the smaller scales in order to have a more comprehensive layout. To the layman it may seem surprising, but for a really satisfactory layout, even in 'OO' gauge, a space of ten feet by six is none too large. Experiments were therefore made with still smaller sizes. 'TT' gauge ($\frac{1}{2}$-inch rail width) made its appearance but did not gain much support from modellers, and, by the 1960s, 'N' gauge ($\frac{3}{8}$-inch) began to attract more attention. A wide range of items is available in this gauge at the time of writing, and an idea of its size may be seen from the fact that two locomotives can be fitted into a matchbox! With these smaller sizes, workable layouts become possible on any table-top, and a very elaborate layout can be set out in a small box-room.

While all this was going on, changes were also taking place in the trains themselves. The familiar four-wheeled locomotives and coaches of previous years failed to satisfy modern children. They demanded locomotives and trains that were recognizable copies of the real thing. A 'free-lance' locomotive which merely bore the label *Royal Scot*, as in pre-war days, was no longer acceptable, and any loco so named had to be a scale model of the real thing or as near as possible to one.

Many of today's locomotives, claimed by their makers to be scale models, are in fact far from being so. It is not within the scope of this book to deal with craftsman-built or even semi-mass produced models, but now, as in former days, such things are available to the rich. Even they are not really scale models in every respect, however. For example, the cab sides of a model loco have to be very much over-scale in thickness in order to be robust enough. Also the length of model locos and the arrangement of the bogie wheels need considerable modification in order to persuade them to negotiate the curves of model systems. Having said all this, however, the author must admit that the model locomotives and trains of today are much nearer to being scale models than were those of his youth.

Another change has been in the material of which model locomotives are constructed. Originally tin-plate was universal, formed and stamped and either painted or lithographed to represent the style and colour required. A post-war trend was the change to die-cast metal, which enabled more detail in relief to be incorporated at reasonable cost. Die-cast locomotives were very common in the 1950s and are still made, but, as might be expected, toy-makers are turning more and more to plastic as their main material.

The final change which we have to consider is in the motive power. When the war came, most commercial model locos were obtainable with either clockwork or electric motors. Clockwork did reappear after the war but it soon became obvious, in the smaller scales at least, that electricity would be the sole means of propulsion. Motors of 12 Volt DC became the standard, because control was easier to install in such a system, and starting, stopping and reversing were much more positive than in AC models of former years. All model electric trains once had a centre rail laid between the running rails and insulated from them. Current was picked up from this rail and returned via the running rails. This system is virtually obsolete now and most makers favour the 'two-rail' system. By ingenious insulation, current is fed to the locomotive through the wheels on one side and returned through the other. Apart from a saving in cost, such systems look more like the real thing. Let us now consider a short history of the different makes and gauges obtainable in the shops since the war, when the trends mentioned above will be discernible.

'O' GAUGE

There is no doubt that the popularity of 'O' gauge was already in decline prior to the outbreak of World War II. With smaller houses and flats with no gardens, locations had become scarce for the large layouts once so common in this gauge. However, several of the firms which were prominent in the 'O' gauge field before the war did make a reappearance.

Hornby once made the most popular 'O' gauge system, and in 1946 and 1947 the firm promised, in its advertisements, a return of the range. Very few of the more elaborate models actually came back, however.

The locomotives that did return were of the small four-wheeled variety, and, although some bogie coaches and wagons were seen for a short time, they were soon withdrawn again. Nevertheless, a fair selection of the simpler items did become available and even some completely new vehicles appeared in the 1950s. Nearly all these items were eventually repainted in British Railways' colours, albeit some time after the real railway colours had been changed. Soon after this, alas, the withdrawal of items gathered speed and the end was in sight. A few of the smallest train sets were available as late as 1967, but by 1969 nothing was left of a once-vast range. Strangely enough, these simple tin-plate trains are now greatly sought-after by collectors, mainly middle-aged men who knew the trains in the days of their glory. In fact a flourishing Hornby Railway Collectors' Association exists whose members show an almost fanatical allegiance to the products of the Hornby factory.

The French Hornby story was a little different. A separate series of trains, Continental in character, was manufactured in pre-war days at a factory near Paris. More of these returned after the war, including a series of electric types, unlike in Britain, where only clockwork trains reappeared. By 1969, however, these French trains were becoming difficult to get, and they have now begun to join their British sisters on the shelves of collectors.

Another firm whose products reappeared in some variety was Bassett-Lowke. Their trains were always in a more expensive category than Hornby's but many of them were nearer to scale models than toys. Several excellent inexpensive models powered by clockwork or electric motors were available in the 1950s and even one simple steam-driven locomotive was listed for a time. Following the death of the founder of the firm, Bassett-Lowke Trains ceased to exist as mass-produced models for boys. However the firm has continued to produce hand-made scale models in 'O' gauge, and these can still be bought by those who can afford the prices, which run into three figures for a single locomotive. At the other end of the scale, there was always a market for very cheap train sets and several manufacturers returned to these after the war. One firm which produced some cheap but creditable clockwork and electric locos was the Birmingham company of Chad Valley.

Very few American-made model railway systems have ever been popular in Great Britain but an exception, for a while, was the firm of Lionel. Their die-cast and plastic electric 'O' gauge trains enjoyed a vogue in the early post-war years but are seldom seen today, though still popular in their native country. They included locos with realistic imitation smoke and ingenious working accessories, but British boys did not seem to be interested, probably because they were so different from the trains with which they were familiar.

To bring the 'O' gauge scene right up to date, mention must be made of the recently introduced Triang 'Big Big' series. These are strongly made of plastic and include several items, for example the track, which are virtually unbreakable. Although intended as toys for younger children, some items, such as the diesel locomotive, are accurate models which appeal to the more mature enthusiast. The locomotives are electrically driven and operated from dry batteries.

'OO' GAUGE

'OO' gauge was first introduced to this country by Bing, and several other makes were available at the beginning of the war. Today it is the most popular of all the gauges and the one for which the widest range of components is available.

Hornby Dublo (pronounced 'double O') came out just before the war and the full range returned afterwards. In fact considerable extensions and changes were made right up to the time the Hornby factory came under the Triang organization. The first post-war Hornby Dublo trains were exactly like their pre-war counterparts except for the couplings, an efficient automatic knuckle coupling replacing the simple pre-war type. Only electric Hornby Dublo trains returned after the war, the previous clockwork range being dropped. At first, Hornby Dublo was a three-rail electric system with die-cast locos and tin-plate trains, but they later went over to a two-rail system and plastic vehicles were introduced. The system was always 12 Volt DC and many working accessories were available.

The only other complete commercial system in the immediate post-war years was that of Trix. This, first introduced in 1935, came from Germany, but British-type trains were later produced in this country. There have been revolutionary changes in the Trix system during the years of its existence and several changes of ownership. At first Trix was a 14 Volt AC system, with a unique device which enabled two trains to run independently on the same track, picking up their current respectively from the two running rails and sharing the centre rail as a common return. This arrangement enabled many interesting operations to be undertaken, but a fault with the original Trix was the unreliable reversing gear in the locomotives. Later Trix cured this by changing to 12 Volt DC, while still retaining the 'twin' system of two trains on one track. More realistic locomotives were made and an excellent track appeared, which had the added advantage of accepting other makes of stock. The latest Trix system is two-rail, with really magnificent models, as can be seen from the plates in this book.

Without doubt, the most comprehensive system at present available in 'OO' gauge is that of Triang. This first appeared in the 1950s with a very simple electric train set for small children made by Rovex. Adopted and improved by Triang, it rapidly expanded into a really comprehensive system, growing more accurate and realistic all the time. This was the first commercial two-rail system, and the same simple basic design first introduced has been followed but with steady improvements in appearance. The Triang system is 12 Volt DC and entirely plastic. When Triang merged with Hornby, the name was changed from Triang Railways to Triang Hornby, and some of the Hornby Dublo items were retained.

Another system, of French parentage, is that of Playcraft (12 Volt DC), and again made of plastic. This is inexpensive, mainly intended for younger boys and marketed throughout Britain by Woolworths. There were and are a good many smaller firms in the 'OO' gauge business but these are mainly makers of kits and components. There are also several foreign manufacturers who provide complete systems, but, as their locomotives are seldom found in Great Britain, they have not been included in this survey.

In the late 1950s, a new size known as 'TT' gauge was launched. It was claimed that because of the more compact nature of this size, satisfactory layouts could be built where 'OO' gauge was too big. Triang brought out quite a comprehensive range of locos, trains and accessories, and a few other manufacturers made kits and components, but somehow it never really caught on. Perhaps this was because it was only slightly smaller than 'OO' gauge or there may have been other reasons. At the time of writing, no ready-made items are left, so, as a commercial alternative, this size is now non-existent.

'N' GAUGE

The most recent size to be made in quantity is the one known as 'N' gauge (N = nine-millimetre or $\frac{3}{8}$-inch rail width). Not long ago only a few private craftsmen had modelled in this tiny size but now several makers—notably Trix of Germany and Lima of Italy—have launched a range of models, most of which are obtainable in Britain. Furthermore they include stock of British, Continental and American design, so an enthusiast in any country can either have just those items which are appropriate to him, or mix in more exotic pieces. The very small size of 'N' gauge means that anyone can find space for a layout. Only one-quarter of the space needed for an 'OO' gauge layout is needed for the same layout in 'N' gauge. An interesting 'N' gauge layout can even fit on to a coffee table! All items in this gauge are 12 Volt DC, two-rail.

THE MODELS

60985
45746
3435
HORNBY
HORNBY
3435

1 HORNBY 'O' GAUGE CLOCKWORK LOCOMOTIVES

In the late 1920s and early 1930s Hornby 'O' gauge was the most popular model railway of all. In fact, in those days people referred to boys' layouts as 'Hornby Trains' whether they were of that make or not!

Top picture: This is the No. 20 locomotive, previously known as the MO. It is an historic loco, as it was the last one produced, was not withdrawn until 1967, and was available in a set as late as Christmas 1968. It was also the smallest ever produced in the Hornby series (eight and a half inches long, with tender). A simple toy engine with hook and loop couplings common to this type, it was well finished and strongly built. It reappeared in 1947 in a finish similar to the pre-war model, red No. 6161 or green No. 2595. In 1954 it was the first Hornby 'O' gauge loco to be changed to BR colours, and this example shows this style. The loco was then numbered 60985 and the serial changed to No. 20. It was always non-reversing. Although, as in most Hornby locomotives, this was a freelance design, the numbers of actual engines were used in order to appeal to the young owner. The number 6161 carried by the red version was actually that of an LMS *Royal Scot* class named *King's Own*. Similarly, No. 2595 was used by a LNER 4-6-2 locomotive named *Trigo*. When colours were changed by BR, Hornby used a fictitious number 60985, near to the numbers on Eastern Region V2 class locomotives.

Second picture: A much more recent locomotive introduced in 1956 in the No. 30 series. It therefore always carried the BR livery shown here and the number 45746. This loco replaced the M1 shown below and was of similar but more up-to-date design. It had a reversing mechanism and was fitted with a combined hook and loop type coupling unique to the No. 30 series. Again, this is a freelance design and number 45746 did not exist on British Railways, but it is near to the numbers carried by LMS *Jubilee* class locomotives.

Third and fourth pictures: The M1 locomotive in the two available colours of red and green. A re-introduction of the pre-war M1, it had only minor differences such as a strengthening plate on the front of the tender. The couplings were of the link type formerly used on all Hornby stock but later only on M1 locos and vehicles. The loco had a powerful reversing mechanism and good specimens now fetch high prices among collectors. These locos had no connection at all with any real engines, and the number 3435 is a serial standing for 1934–35, the date of the last design change in the model. (All models are from the Author's collection)

3
82011
L N E R
460
2270
L M S

2 HORNBY 'O' GAUGE CLOCKWORK TANK LOCOMOTIVES

The locos shown on the previous page were of a simpler and cheaper type from the rest of the Hornby range. We now come to the standard series, and illustrate first the only tank locomotive type produced after the war. This was known as the M3 in pre-war days but was re-designated the 101 in 1947. At first it was available in all four companies' colours, LMS, LNER, GW and SR, but from about 1950 only LMS and LNER finishes were produced. The main identification points of a post-war loco are the larger chimney and the centre lamp bracket over the front coupling. It was standard practice to fit all standard Hornby locos with link couplings on the front and automatic ones on the rear, as on these locos. As on all the larger engines, a powerful reversing mechanism was fitted and the wheels were coupled. The three locos shown on this page are identical except for finish.

Top picture: This shows the loco in BR black, No. 82011. It was known as No. 40 and was the first post-war Hornby engine to appear in black livery. The last style before deletion was similar except that the new BR emblem replaced the 'lion and wheel' shown. The number 82011 carried by this locomotive was that of a BR Class 3 2-6-2 tank, used mainly on local passenger trains.

Second picture: The livery here is LNER green No. 460 and serial 101. There may have been an alternative finish with the No. 7602, and the author would be very interested to hear of one of these, as it would be extremely rare. The number 460 was the same as that on the real LNER 0-6-2 tank engines of the N7 class formerly used mainly on suburban services from King's Cross.

Third picture: This shows the 101 tank loco in LMS finish and numbered 2270. This and the LNER finish were identical with the pre-war liveries. The red loco in this series has the number 2270 and this is believed to be that of an old Tilbury Railway passenger tank loco.

(All the models on this page are from the Author's collection)

L M S
5600
50153
L N E R
1842
60199

3 HORNBY 'O' GAUGE CLOCKWORK TENDER LOCOMOTIVES

The largest Hornby post-war locomotive is shown here in the four finishes in which it was available.

This loco was the No. 1 of pre-war days, and again minor changes were made when it was re-introduced, such as a centre bottom lamp bracket on both front and rear and a larger chimney. The reversing mechanism was of a type superior to that fitted to the 101 tank and so the locos shown on this page were the most powerful available in post-war years. For a short time, and for export sales only, this loco was available with an electric mechanism, the only one so fitted to be made in Britain. In the catalogue of 1948, this locomotive was offered in all four company colours, but it is doubtful if any except LMS and LNER actually appeared.

Top picture: The loco is shown as a 501 in LMS red and numbered 5600. This and the LNER version below were unique in having a flat matt finish, only used between 1948 and 1956 (when colours were changed to BR) and only applied to this loco. Again this is a freelance design, although these more elaborate Hornby locomotives had features which resembled engines of the LNER. The number carried by the red version, however, is from an LMS *Jubilee* class locomotive named *Bermuda*.

Second picture: This shows the locomotive in BR green finish, serial No. 51 and numbered 50153. This fictitious number 50153 was probably a serial code for a 501 loco designed in 1953.

Third picture: This is the counterpart of the loco in the top picture but numbered 1842 and finished in LNER green. This loco does share a number with a real engine; in this case a LNER K3 class 2-6-0.

Fourth picture: Serial No. 50 in this finish, the loco is shown as BR black No. 60199. The number on this loco does not relate to a real locomotive nor does it appear to be a serial number.

(All the models on this page are from the Author's collection)

S.N.C.F.
BB-8051
8051
3615
3615
2528

4 FRENCH HORNBY 'O' GAUGE CLOCKWORK LOCOMOTIVES

The French Hornby factory at Bobigny has always produced an independent range of locomotives and trains, although some items were very similar to their British opposite numbers. After the war the factory made a much larger range of 'O' gauge items than in this country, including electrically operated models and some larger bogie locos and rolling stock. Those shown on this page are all clockwork locos which are non-reversing, and come within the French 'M' series. They are, however, more detailed and elaborate models than the British 'M' series.

Top picture: A 'BB' loco in SNCF livery and numbered 8051. This was a clockwork model of an electric prototype. It had features unlike those on British Hornby engines—for example, buffers on the front and not on the back, and vice versa with the coupling. The brake lever, not seen in the picture, protrudes from the side instead of from the end as on British types. It is a very pleasing model with a wealth of detail for a simple tin-plate locomotive.

Second picture: The *Express* loco, which is rather like the British MO, finished in a handsome livery of red and green and numbered 3615. Typical French practice is followed by the dropped front end and smoke deflectors. The loco looks quaint because it has a representation of outside cylinders but no coupling or connecting rods.

Third picture: The French 'M' loco, which bears some resemblance to the British M1. This has more detail than the *Express* and is slightly larger. Like the 'BB', it has buffers only at the front and a coupling only at the rear. The tender is very similar to the British M1 but numbered 2528.

These are all freelance locomotives bearing no resemblance in numbering or style to engines on the real French Railways.

(All the models on this page are from the Author's collection)

RUSTON
Blue Flier
3D95

5 TRIANG 'BIG BIG' 'O' GAUGE ELECTRIC LOCOMOTIVES

This is the latest gauge 'O' system to be introduced, made of plastic and electrically operated from dry batteries carried in the locomotives. Although intended primarily as a toy for young children, the system contains some items which are quite near to scale models.

Top picture: A simple steam locomotive, based on an industrial type. It is brightly coloured, sturdy and the modern counterpart of the tin engine of years ago. The top is removable in order to change the batteries. Control is by means of a lever on the side which selects forward, stop and reverse, and can be operated by a remote trip.

Second picture: A diesel shunter which has the same base and 'works' as the loco above but a different body. These two locos are considerably overscale for gauge 'O', but exactness of scale is not important in a toy system of this sort. It is more to the point that each item should be robust and foolproof, as these locos are.

Third picture: Although in the same series, this representation of a BR *Hymek* diesel locomotive is virtually a scale model except for minor details like the name *Blue Flyer*. Many of these locomotives have been improved and modified by serious modellers to run on their systems.

(All the models on this page are shown by courtesy of Messrs Bold and Burrows of St Albans)

80033
46232
DUCHESS OF MONTROSE
48158
60030
GOLDEN FLEECE
L N E R
4498
SIR NIGEL GRESLEY
7032
DENBIGH CASTLE

6 HORNBY DUBLO 'OO' GAUGE ELECTRIC LOCOMOTIVES

Top picture: BR 2-6-4 tank locomotive No. 80033. This shows the two-rail version. The earlier three-rail one was numbered 80054, and this loco was unusual in that it incorporated a speed device in the cab. This is a model of the BR 2-6-4 tank used all over British Railways for passenger service until replaced by diesels in 1962 to 1966.

Second picture: BR (LMR) 4-6-2 locomotive *Duchess of Montrose* No. 46232 (three-rail). The original version was *Duchess of Atholl* No. 6231 in LMS red. Then came the loco shown, followed by *City of Liverpool* in three-rail and *City of London* in two-rail, both finished in BR red and both having slight modifications to their body-work. The *Duchess* class locomotives, on which this model is based, were a famous class built by the LMS shortly before the war for service between London and Scotland on the Euston route. Some were at one time streamlined and one, named *Coronation*, was painted in garter blue for the coronation of King George VI.

Third picture: BR (LMR) 2-8-0 freight locomotive No. 48158 (three-rail). The two-rail version was numbered 48109. This was one of the most powerful model locomotives made in this country. The real loco was an LMS design built in the late 1930s. Many of them were sent on active service in Europe and the Middle East during World War II.

Fourth and fifth pictures: These show two different versions of the oldest locomotive in the Hornby series, the 4-6-2 A4 class of the former LNER, a model first produced in pre-war days. In picture 4 we see the two-rail version No. 60030 *Golden Fleece,* the three-rail version of which was No. 60022 *Mallard.*In one way this was the most famous of all British locomotives, because the real *Mallard* still holds the world speed record for steam locos (126 mph in 1938). These engines were used on the LNER route to Scotland from King's Cross. Picture 5 shows the loco in its original form as No. 4498 *Sir Nigel Gresley* in LNER blue.

Sixth picture: BR (WR) 4-6-0 locomotive No. 7032 *Denbigh Castle* (two-rail). The three-rail version was 7013 *Bristol Castle.* The real *Castle* class locomotives had a long life. Originally built in the 1920s by the Great Western Railways, they were still being built in 1950 under BR ownership. They hauled important trains on the Western Region.

(All the models on this page are shown by courtesy of Mr G. C. Buttress, except for No. 5, the property of Master Andrew Riisnaes)

4008
TRI-ANG RAILWAYS
D 9012
G W R

7 RIVAL DIESELS AND A STRANGER

All 'OO' gauge locomotives on this page are 12 Volt DC two-rail, now accepted as the standard system for virtually all model locomotives.

Top picture: Triang Transcontinental Series, main-line diesel. This is a model of a typical American diesel locomotive made by Triang for this series. Supplied mainly for export, the series contains steam and diesel locomotives based on American and Canadian practice, together with suitable coaches and wagons. The model shown is freelance, but it has the usual American headlamp (which actually lights up) and, in contrast to British trains, no buffers are fitted.

Second picture: Hornby Dublo BR diesel electric locomotive No. D 9012 *Crepello*. This was one of the first model diesel locos made, originally in a three-rail version without a name. It is a model of the *Deltic* diesel loco, the most powerful in use on British Railways. Developing 3300 bhp, the *Deltic* is capable of speeds in excess of 100 mph.

Third picture: Graham Farish GWR pannier tank loco No. 9410. One of the smaller independent manufacturers, Graham Farish have produced some interesting locomotives over the years. The earlier ones looked more realistic than their contemporaries but had inferior motors. Their latest locos, like the one shown, have first-class mechanisms and are also accurate scale models. The real GWR pannier tanks were once to be seen in very large numbers on shunting duties in all parts of the West Country. Then, like all other steam locos, they were rapidly broken up when diesel shunters replaced them.

(All the models on this page are shown by courtesy of Mr G. C. Buttress)

85
1168
L M S
60103

8 TRIX 'OO' GAUGE ELECTRIC LOCOMOTIVES (14 VOLT AC)

The locos shown on this page are of the type used on the original 'Trix Twin' railway, which was quite different to any other system. It was called 'twin' because two trains could run independently on the same track, as described earlier. The mechanisms were sturdy and powerful but the reversing mechanisms were somewhat temperamental, to say the least! They operated by a sequence device and not by reversing the current as in DC systems, and many people felt that this fault spoilt an otherwise excellent railway. Trix later changed to a 12 Volt DC system, but locos of the original type are still sought by collectors and operators.

Top picture: The original Trix tank locomotive, in this case No. 85 in BR black, but numerous different colours and numbers were used over the years. There was a similar tender version of this loco, both being of freelance design.

Second picture: LMS 4-4-0 compound locomotive No. 1168. This loco also carried various numbers and was available in LMS red and later in BR black. Apart from the size of the wheels, it was a good representation of the real locomotive. Very early post-war Trix locos and stock were fitted with Continental-type couplings as used in pre-war days, but the locos shown on this page have the British knuckle-type automatic couplings.

Third picture: BR (ER) 4-6-2 locomotive No. 60103 *Scotsman*. This is also a good representation of the real loco except that for some reason Trix named it *Scotsman* instead of *Flying Scotsman*. This engine had a remote-controlled uncoupling device on the tender. The colour was originally BR blue, a style applied to very few model locos because it lasted only a short time on the actual railways.

(Models in pictures 1 and 2 are shown by courtesy of Mr R. P. Riisnaes and that in picture 3 by courtesy of Mr G. C. Buttress)

73000
70000

9 TRIX 'OO' GAUGE ELECTRIC LOCOMOTIVES (12 VOLT DC)

Following a change of ownership in the late 1950s, major changes were made to the Trix system. Completely new locos appeared which were accurate models of the real thing, and they were powered by 12 Volt DC motors which eliminated the previous reversing troubles. The superb detail of these die-cast models make them sought today by enthusiasts, as they were discontinued when a further change of ownership caused Trix to revise their range again.

Top picture: BR Class five Standard 4-6-0 No. 73000. This loco was available in either green or black and could be adapted for either two-rail or three-rail running. This is a model of one of the last steam locos built by BR at Doncaster and used on both passenger and goods trains.

Second picture: BR (WR) 0-6-2 tank locomotive No. 6664. This was also available in two-rail or three-rail versions and in green or black. The colour variation on this and the above loco was not really in accordance with actual practice, but such liberties in colours have always been taken in the model railway world, as locos produced only in the colours of the real ones would have a drab appearance. This is a model of one of the older GW 0-6-2 tanks used mainly on coal trains in South Wales.

Third picture: BR Standard 4-6-2 locomotive No. 70000, *Britannia*. A magnificent model of this famous locomotive, probably the best commercially available. The massive appearance and detail on tender and cab, in this and in the loco in the top picture, can be seen by studying the photograph. The real *Britannias* were the last top-class express steam locomotives built by BR, and they could be found all over the country from Glasgow to Penzance.

(All the models on this page are shown by courtesy of Mr G. C. Buttress)

BARNSTAPLE
34005
31340

10 BRITISH AND CONTINENTAL LOCOMOTIVES

Models of French and German locomotives and trains have always been available in this country in limited numbers. Some of these are the products of Continental firms while others are made by British manufacturers. It is therefore not uncommon to find layouts which mainly follow British practice but which have a few Continental items running on them. Two such locos are illustrated on this page and, like the British-style ones shown, are both 12 Volt DC two-rail in 'OO' gauge.

Top picture: Triang/Wrenn BR (SR) 4-6-2 locomotive No. 34005 *Barnstaple*. This is a die-cast model of a former Hornby Dublo locomotive now made for Triang by Wrenn. It is shown here pulling a train of Pullman coaches, the sort of duty these locos were used for in real life. The actual locomotive belongs to a series which was rebuilt by British Railways from the streamlined *West Country* class of the former Southern Railways. In this form they resembled the *Britannia* class locomotives and undertook the heaviest and fastest duties on the Southern Region in the late 1950s and early 1960s.

Second picture: Playcraft SNCF 2-8-2 freight locomotive. This magnificent model of a massive freight locomotive is made by the French firm of Jouef and sold in Britain by Playcraft. Other Playcraft items are mainly of the simple inexpensive type, but this is a detailed scale model with a high-quality mechanism which is unusual in that the tender is powered and not the locomotive. The real loco is used on the French State Railways for hauling heavy goods trains.

Third picture: Triang 2-6-2 Continental tank locomotive. This loco, while being of freelance design, is based on the type used on the German railways. The plain black body and red underframe and wheels are typical of German practice. The real locos of this type are still used on both passenger and goods trains.

Fourth picture: Triang/Wrenn BR (SR) 0-6-0 tank locomotive No. 31340. This model was produced towards the end of the Hornby Dublo era and later re-issued by Wrenn for Triang. It is a model of a shunting loco used by the former Southern Railways. Locos of this type were also used on boat trains from Folkestone harbour to the main station, a heavy task which sometimes called for three locos to be used together. (All the models on this page are shown by courtesy of Messrs Bold & Burrows of St Albans)

C R
60103
FLYING SCOTSMAN
46200
THE PRINCESS ROYAL
34051

11 TRIANG 'OO' GAUGE ELECTRIC LOCOMOTIVES (12 VOLT DC)

The growth of Triang Railways (now Triang Hornby) began as late as 1954. The system now offers the railway modeller the largest range of British type models currently available. The system was developed from the Rovex Train Set (a crude plastic toy by modern standards) which Triang took over and used as a foundation to build upon. Later on, when Hornby was merged with Triang, some of the Hornby Dublo locos were retained and are still available, but are now built for Triang by Wren.

Top picture: Caledonian Railways 4-2-2 locomotive No. 123. This is a model of an old-time locomotive, which in real life is preserved by British Rail for exhibition purposes. Triang have introduced models of several such locomotives, such as the *Lord of the Isles* and Stephenson's *Rocket*, but only the latter is currently available.

Second picture: BR (ER) 4-6-2 locomotive No. 60103 *Flying Scotsman*. Perhaps the real *Flying Scotsman* was the most famous locomotive ever built and it certainly captured the imagination of every boy of the author's generation. The real one has been preserved in working order by a private enthusiast. The photograph shows the model in BR finish, but an alternative version is available in the old LNER colours and fitted with the famous corridor tender.

Third picture: BR (LMR) 4-6-2 locomotive No. 46200 *The Princess Royal*. This is a modified version of the original Rovex locomotive from which Triang Railways were developed. The photograph shows the model in its latest form but other versions have existed in black as *Princess Victoria* and in green as *Princess Elizabeth*. The original loco was also *Princess Elizabeth* but coloured black, and there have been several changes in the body and the mechanism since then. The *Princess* class locomotives were built by the LMS between 1933 and 1935. One of this class, *Princess Elizabeth*, averaged 70 mph on the journey to Scotland and was the first loco to do so.

Fourth picture BR (SR) 4-6-2 locomotive No. 34051 *Winston Churchill*. This model is based on a loco of a revolutionary and controversial design which appeared on the Southern Railway during the war. The model is also available in Southern finish named *Biggin Hill*, *Hurricane* or *Fighter Command*. The real locos of this class were the first genuinely streamlined steam locos to be built in this country.

(All models are shown by courtesy of Mr G. C. Buttress)

7
NELLIE
D2907
748
30027

12 TRIANG 'OO' GAUGE ELECTRIC LOCOMOTIVES (12 VOLT DC)

This page shows some of the smaller locomotives in the Triang range, including a very old one which is no longer available.

Top picture: 0-4-0 Industrial tank locomotive No. 7 *Nellie*. A most attractive loco, freelance in design, but closely resembling many of the shunting engines owned by private firms. Alternative versions were available in red named *Polly* and in yellow named *Connie*.

Second picture: BR 0-4-0 diesel shunter No. D2907. Shown here in BR green livery, this loco is now obtainable in red finish with Army markings in the Triang 'Battle Space' series.

Third picture: Freelance 0-6-0 saddle tank locomotive No. 748. These locos are called 'saddle tanks' because the water tank is on top of the boiler instead of in the more usual position at the sides. This model is one of the earliest in the Triang range and was once obtainable with a clockwork mechanism.

Fourth picture: BR (SR) 0-4-4 tank locomotive No. 30027. A recent model and a very realistic and pleasing one. A comparison of this picture with the previous one gives some idea of the improvements which have been made to Triang locos over the years. A special and unique feature of this particular model is the 'glowing firebox' and boiler tubes seen through the opening smokebox door.

(All the models on this page are shown by courtesy of Mr G. C. Buttress)

SLEEPING CAR
D 801
SPARTAN
D844
WESTERN VISCOUNT
D1046

13 DIESELS ALL!

With the inevitable replacing of steam locomotives by diesels, toy-makers were not long in producing models of this type. Here we see a selection of such models, again all 'OO' gauge 12 Volt DC, two-rail.

Top picture: Triang BR *Inter-city* diesel Pullman train. Finished in the latest BR style, this train represents in model form the ultimate in luxury travel. The real diesel Pullmans were originally used between St Pancras and Manchester, but they have since been transferred to the Western Region.

Second and third pictures: Trix *Warship* class diesel locomotives No. D801 *Vanguard,* and D844 *Spartan.* These modern locomotives are produced by Trix in three different colours each with a different name. They are models of the 2200-bhp diesel locomotives used on South Wales expresses.

Fourth picture: Trix *Western* class diesel electric locomotive No. D1045 *Western Viscount.* A recent Trix production obtainable in three different colours but with no less than six different names. More powerful than the *Warship* class with a rating of 2700 bhp the real locos pull the fastest expresses on the Western Region.

Fifth picture: Triang Transcontinental Series 'double-ended' diesel loco. Although freelance in design, this model is based on a type of locomotive used on the Victorian Railways of Australia.

(All the models on this page are shown by courtesy of Messrs Bold & Burrows of St Albans)

Haig
1A20
27000

14 DIESEL, ELECTRIC AND STEAM

Although diesel now reigns supreme on British Railways, with also an increasing mileage of electric trains, most modellers include at least some steam locomotives among their stock. In this picture we see all three types of motive power together.

Top picture: Triang BR (LMR) 0-6-0 tank locomotive No. 47606. This was one of the first locomotives designed by Triang and produced in 1952. It was also the first loco to be fitted with a smoke generator, an ingenious device which produces artificial smoke from capsules as the loco is driven along. The picture shows the loco pulling a short goods train, the kind of duty once performed by them in actual service, although they occasionally undertook passenger haulage as well.

Second picture: Triang BR *Hymek* diesel locomotive No. D7063. This is a model of a BR diesel locomotive used all over the system for pulling both passenger and goods trains. An alternative version of this model, produced by Wren, has a working two-tone horn.

Third picture: Playcraft BR D6100 class mixed traffic diesel locomotive. Yet another one of the many types of BR diesel locos, shown in this picture with a train of Playcraft Continental-type wagons. This is a powerful model with all eight wheels driven.

Fourth picture: Triang BR EM2 electric locomotive No. E27000, *Electra*. An interesting model which, like the real thing, can be made to pick up current from an overhead-wire system. Alternatively, as shown in the picture, it can be run on normal two-rail track in the usual way. Real locomotives of this type are used on British Railways on recently electrified lines such as that from Euston to Manchester, Sheffield and Liverpool.

(All the models on this page are shown by courtesy of Messrs Bold & Burrows of St Albans)

2
ZILLERTAL
III
IV
IV

15 'N' GAUGE LOCOMOTIVES AND COACHES

Although at the time of writing, 'N' gauge is not followed by many modellers, its popularity is increasing and a wider range of items is becoming available, mainly of Continental design and all 12 Volt DC two-rail.

Top and second pictures: Minitrix German 0-6-0 tank locomotive and coaches. This charming model is freelance but based on a vintage German design once used on branch lines. An idea of the size of 'N' gauge can be seen when one realizes that this loco is just two inches long! Minitrix, a German manufacturer, have a comprehensive system including British, Continental and American style trains, but, as yet, few of these items have been imported into this country in any quantity.

Third and fourth pictures: Lilliput OO/N 0-6-2 tank locomotive and Eggerbahn coaches. These items, although running on 'N' gauge track, are larger than 'N' gauge and are made to the same scale as 'OO' gauge to represent real 'Narrow Gauge' lines. The charm of such 'way-out' railways attracts quite a following among enthusiasts, and those in Britain which open during the summer season are always crowded. The advantages of modelling in this scale are freedom to do as one pleases, and the fact that many items designed for 'OO' gauge can be used.

Mobil
PENNSYLVANIA
383

16 MAIN-LINE TRAINS IN 'N' GAUGE

The Italian firm of Lima produce an excellent range of 'N' gauge items which, in this country, are sold under the Wrenn label. This picture shows three trains mainly made up from these items, and once again all are 12 Volt DC two-rail.

First picture (left foreground): Wrenn/Lima 'N' gauge American Pennsylvanian Railways 2-6-4 tank loco No. 383. The front view of this model shows the differences between it and the British one next to it. The former has a typical cow-catcher open frame, and various 'ironmongery' all over the body. It has remarkable detail for such a small model but the picture shows it in an impossible situation—pulling two Continental tank wagons and a British Freightliner!

Second picture: Wrenn/Lima 'N' gauge BR 2-6-4 tank locomotive No. 80033. A model of the standard BR mixed traffic tank used on all sections before the diesels took over. This model has the same prototype as the Hornby Dublo tank engine shown on a previous page and, strangely enough, also the same number! It is shown pulling two Minitrix WR coaches.

Third picture: We could not resist another shot of the German tank loco shown on the previous page. This time the excellent detail on the top of the loco can clearly be seen, but the WR full-size coach seems too heavy for it!

(All the models on this and the preceding page are shown by courtesy of Messrs Bold & Burrows of St Albans)

This is briefly the story so far. What of the future? It would take a bold man to predict the next twenty years of model railways but the author feels they will still be with us after that time. Model cars are, of course, a challenge, and these are now available in great profusion, from simple die-cast models to large six- or eight-lane racing circuits. Yet fascinating though these may be, trains still hold their own. Strangely enough too, the latest trains include a fair sprinkling of old steam models. The fact that locos were once steam-driven and can still represent steam in miniature gives us the clue to the continuing popularity of model railways. For there is a glamour and a magic about steam that has always been irresistible to men and boys. A steam loco is a live thing with a character and a personality.

The author has owned and loved model locomotives and their trains for over forty years and has watched the changing scene all that time. He freely admits that his favourites, first, last and for all time are Hornby clockwork tin-plate models, and for him the thrill of seeing and owning these grows more, not less, as he passes through middle age. If these pictures have given something of this pleasure to the reader, the task of compiling and writing about them will have been well worth while.

APPENDIX

Details of the various makes of locomotive included in this book

Make	Gauge	Type of motive power	Material	Whether still available (1970)
Hornby	'O'	Clockwork	Tin-plate	No
French Hornby	'O'	Clockwork	Tin-plate	No
Triang 'Big Big'	'O'	Electric battery-driven 6 Volt DC	Plastic	Yes
Hornby Dublo	'OO'	Electric 12 Volt DC, two- and three-rail	Die-cast	No
Trix	'OO'	Electric 14 Volt AC 'Twin'	Die-cast	No
		12 Volt DC, two- and three-rail		Yes
Triang/ Hornby	'OO'	Electric 12 Volt DC,	Plastic	Yes
Triang/ Wrenn	'OO'	two-rail	Die-cast	Yes
Graham Farish	'OO'	Electric 12 Volt DC, two-rail	Die-cast	Yes
Playcraft	'OO'	Electric 12 Volt DC, two-rail	Plastic	Yes
Minitrix	'N'	Electric 12 Volt DC, two-rail	Plastic	Yes

Wrenn/ Lima	'N'	Electric 12 Volt DC, two-rail	Plastic	Yes
Lilliput	'OO/N'	Electric 12 Volt DC, two-rail	Plastic	Yes

INDEX

V

W

THE TROY MODEL CLUB

In the last few years the amount of interest shown in models of all kinds has grown fantastically. The variety and number produced by manufacturers has barely kept up with the demand. Often they are not so much toys but highly accurate and detailed scale miniatures. Yet the length of time any particular model stays in production is often very limited. Surprisingly, books recording this world boom have been few and far between and have seldom shown models in colour.

The Troy Model Club Series has been launched in order to fill this need. Each volume will be illustrated only in colour and will deal with the development and history of popular ranges of models in Britain, Europe and the U.S.A. Well-known specialists have agreed to write for the series.

We would like everyone interested in models to become a member of the club and to tell us what variety of models they want to see covered in future volumes. There is no age limit. We are catering equally for the under-ten's, the over-ten's, their fathers and their grandfathers.

Our concern has been with manufactured models and those made from plastic kits, because this appears to be where the need for books is greatest. Later, we hope to publish volumes which will include individual models constructed by the knowledgeable enthusiast.

The first four books in the series are:

VETERAN AND VINTAGE CARS Cecil Gibson

COMMERCIAL VEHICLES Cecil Gibson

OLDER LOCOMOTIVES (1900-42) P. G. Gomm

RECENT LOCOMOTIVES (1947-70) P. E. Randall

Many other volumes are in preparation.

The launching of the Troy Model Club will be exciting news for everyone who buys, borrows, studies and collects models, for model engineering clubs, for schools, libraries, toy shops and even manufacturers! For membership of the Club, complete the form on the jacket of this book and send it to:

The Secretary The Troy Model Club 36 Park Street London W 1

OTHER TITLES IN THE SERIES NOW AVAILABLE

OLDER LOCOMOTIVES (1900-42) P. G. Gomm

In *Older Locomotives* P. G. Gomm recaptures an era when these brightly coloured models—powered by clockwork, electricity, and even methylated spirits—reflected the excitement of the rapidly developing world of the real locomotives. The superb colour plates show the whole range of models, from the primitive brass-plated contraptions of chimney, boiler and pistons to the sleek *Silver Link, Royal Scot* and *Silver Jubilee*.

SBN 17 213208 8

VETERAN AND VINTAGE CARS Cecil Gibson

Dr Gibson is a lively and knowledgeable guide to the story of the models of veteran and vintage cars *and* the originals they represent. Beautifully made and painted, and accurate to the last detail, such models have become collectors' items, faithfully mirroring the simple mechanism of the veteran cars, the stateliness of the Edwardians and the tremendous technical advances made during the vintage decade after World War I. The whole history of motoring is here available in miniature in superb colour plates.

SBN 17 213206 1

COMMERCIAL VEHICLES Cecil Gibson

Dr Gibson's lively text outlines the development of the commercial vehicle, from the small, squat shapes early in this century to the sleek vans and vast tankers and carriers of today, and from steam carriage to Routemaster. As can be seen in the plates of this book, some models are small bursts of colour, with delightful decals added to their bright paintwork advertising tea, biscuits, newspapers, petrol and many other proprietary goods.

SBN 17 213207 X

All 210 x 149 mm 64 pp 16 colour plates with 4-colour laminated jacket.

ALSO COMING SHORTLY

RACING AND RECORD CARS Cecil Gibson

Dr Gibson outlines the fascinating development of racing cars, rally cars, sports cars and record-breaking cars, from the 130-hp Fiat that won the 1907 French Grand Prix to Graham Hill's Lotus 49B, and from Sir Henry Segrave's 1929 *Golden Arrow* to Donald Campbell's ill-fated *Bluebird*. The colour plates show that the models, like their full-size counterparts, are brightly painted, carry a suggestion of speed and power, and are often extremely beautiful.

SBN 17 213210 X

MILITARY VEHICLES Jack Wheldon

It would be very hard to find any-one who has not at some time fallen under the spell of military models. In *Military Vehicles* Jack Wheldon describes the growth of mechanized armour from World War I to the present day, and the way its spectacular growth has affected battle strategy. The plates show a fascinating variety of tanks, self-propelled guns, lorries, missile-launchers and amphibious vehicles, and make these miniatures delightfully real to us.

SBN 17 213211 8

TROY MODEL CLUB SERIES · TROY MODEL CLUB SERIES · TROY MODEL CLUB SERIES